CONTENTS

INTRODUCTION

If you are looking for garden plants with outstandingly beautiful flowers, rhododendrons and azaleas are among the most spectacular. The range of colour is unequalled, the quantity of flower on each bush is staggering, and the shapes of the flowers are charmingly varied. To add to all these merits, they are easily grown, need little care, and can be obtained in heights varying from tiny shrublets to trees 9m (30ft) and more tall.

K3

RHODODENDRONS AND AZALEAS

ANN BONAR

COLLINS

Editors Maggie Daykin, Susanne Mitchell
Designer Chris Walker
Production Controller Craig Chubb
Picture research Moira McIlroy

First published 1989 by
William Collins Sons & Co Ltd
London · Glasgow · Sydney
Auckland · Toronto · Johannesburg

British Library Cataloguing in Publication Data

Bonar, Ann
    Rhododendrons and azaleas.
    1. Gardens.
    I. Title
    635.9'3362

ISBN 0-00-412-443-X

Typeset by Litho Link Ltd., Welshpool, Powys, Wales
Printed and bound in Hong Kong by Dai Nippon Printing
Company

Front cover: Rhododendron 'Blue Diamond' by The Harry Smith
Horticultural Photographic Collection
Back cover: Japanese Azaleas by Michael Warren

Rhododendron 'Lady Chamberlain' has lovely, narrow bell-shaped flowers, the colours of which range from deep pinkish-red to apricot. And as it tends to grow only to about 2.4m (8ft) and spreads rather less than that, it is an ideal choice for small gardens.

The genus is native to the Himalayas and the Far East, and practically all of those grown in cultivation come from these regions, where they mostly grow in woodland or forests where the shade is dappled, or in sites where they receive at least a little shade each day. However, it is perfectly possible to grow them in a sunny place. They probably won't last in bloom as long, though, and their watering needs watching more carefully.

Rhododendrons are always evergreen, another bonus, so that they furnish the garden in winter, rather than leaving you looking at brown soil and bare branches. The choice of size is extremely wide and, whether you are searching for something to fill a niche on the rock garden, a space in the border, or a gap in a woodland planting, there will always be a beautiful variety to fill it. There are even some prostrate creeping rhododendrons, amazing for a genus which also contains *Rhododendron arboreum,* up to 12m (40ft) in the wild, or *R. grande,* to 9m (30ft).

The flowers of rhododendrons are basically a tubular shape, opening out into a mouth with petal-like edges, but there are all sorts of variations on this theme. Perfect bell shapes, ornamented with frilly petals at the mouth; great spectacular trumpets 10cm (4in) long, funnels with wide open mouths, narrow tubes and tiny, apparently star-like, flowers. Whatever the shape the flowers are carried in clusters, often having ten or more flowers, profusely produced all over the plant, mainly in spring. But if you choose carefully you can have rhododendrons in flower from mid winter to late summer.

RIGHT A cheering bright red, *Azalea* 'Ima-shojo' justifies its place in the collection chosen by plant collector E.H. Wilson.

BELOW *Azalea* 'Hinode-no-taka' has crimson flowers with striking red anthers. Another plant featured in Wilson's famous selection.

Azaleas which, botanically speaking, are also rhododendrons, can be evergreen or deciduous, and are much smaller and more delicate shrubs altogether. Their leaves are smaller and thinner, and their flowers are nearly always tubular or funnel shaped. Some azaleas are scented — as are some of the rhododendrons. The height of these twiggy shrubs ranges between 45cm and 2.4m (18in-8ft); most of them are round about 90-150cm (3-5ft), and the smaller ones make ideal container or patio plants.

A particularly pretty group contains the Kurume azaleas, a collection of 50 which were chosen by the plant collector E. H. Wilson from the thousands he found growing in Japanese nurseries, and which he introduced in 1919. Kurume is a town on the southernmost of the four largest Japanese islands, and was a centre for growing and hybridizing azaleas in the early years of this century. Unlike the majority of the genus, this group need a position in full sun.

SOILS AND PLANTING

The woodlands and forests in which many of this genus are found grow in soil which contains a great deal of rotted organic matter, chiefly in the form of leafmould. This has the effect of making or keeping the soil acid in its reaction, and also ensures that it is well drained and somewhat sponge-like.

Evergreen azaleas, their tightly packed, richly coloured flowers thriving on the plentiful leafmould to be found in woodlands.

Acid soil In order to grow rhododendrons well, you need a garden soil which is acid; those which contain chalk or which are alkaline to any degree will not be suitable. You can try to grow rhododendrons in them, but it will mean regular and expensive additions of sequestrated iron to enable them to absorb iron and prevent the yellowing of their leaves, stunted growth and lack of flowering.

Alternatively, you can make pockets of acid soil in the ground and plant into these, but in time alkaline water will seep in. Or else you can grow them in containers filled with ericaceous compost (the genus belongs to the family *Ericaceae*, which also contains heaths and heathers), which is specially formulated to have an acid reaction. To discover whether the soil is suitably acid, use a simple soil-testing kit, obtainable from garden centres.

Organic matter The garden soil should also contain plenty of rotted organic matter; if the planting site is woodland, it should naturally be of this kind. If not, the lack is easily remedied by the addition of bulky organics such as 'Forest Bark' Ground and Composted Bark, rotted garden compost, peat, leafmould or spent mushroom compost.

Adaptability Good drainage is another important point, and so is moisture but, in fact, most acid soils are well drained and contain organic matter — the exceptions are some clay soils. Most rhododendrons adapt well to varying degrees of acidity, organic matter content and water levels. Their fibrous roots do not spread deeply or widely, hence their vulnerability to surface drying out but, paradoxically, bad subsoil drainage is not so limiting as it might be to a deeply rooting shrub.

Preparation for planting For planting in beds, borders, shrubberies, woodlands and lawns, dig a hole 30-60cm (1-2ft) wide and deep, keeping the topsoil separate; this can be 5-80cm (2-24in) deep on average and is crumbly and easily dug. Fork up the soil at the base of the hole and then mix bulky organic matter with it, and return the dug-out soil — also mixed with the same material — adding about half as much as the soil. If it is already fairly rich in humus content, do not use so much, and vice versa.

Soils which are particularly well drained, such as the sandy or shingly kinds, are likely to be short of nutrients, and fertilizer dressings will be essential. The best planting times are autumn and spring. If planting in autumn, mix in a bonemeal dressing at about 112g/sq m (4oz/sq yd). For spring plantings in early and mid spring, also mix in a slow-acting, organic, nitrogenous fertilizer such as hoof-and-horn at the same rate, thoroughly and evenly mixed with the returned soil.

CHOOSING AND BUYING

Garden Centres You can obtain rhododendrons from your local garden centre, nearly always in containers made of various materials, the most common being black plastic sheet. You can also get them from DIY chain stores, garden shops and general chain stores which have a garden department, but the best selection will be from the garden centres – the bigger the centre, the wider the choice.

Mail-order Nurseries You can also buy them mail-order from nurseries, some of which specialize in rhododendrons and azaleas. Plants obtained from these nurseries will generally be 'balled', that is, will have a ball of fine fibrous roots, usually wrapped in hessian, plastic or similar material. Ideally, these should be planted between early and the middle of late autumn and, to ensure that you get what you want, when you want it, order well in advance, in early or mid summer, from the catalogue that such nurseries supply.

What to look for The advantage of garden centres is that you can see what you are buying; you can be certain that you are getting the variety you want, and you can see all sorts of rhododendrons and azaleas in various shapes and sizes. You can plant them as soon as you get them home, too, but a word of warning here: planting in hot dry weather in summer makes it difficult for them to establish well, even if you have taken every possible care in the preparation of the ground and keep a really close watch on watering requirements.

When you are buying plants on the spot, look for those with plenty of good dark green leaves, and plenty of flower bud, if spring-time. Avoid specimens with pale or yellowing foliage, or whose leaves are spotted or marked in any way.

PLANTING

If you have ordered plants from a nursery, and they have arrived during an autumn which is dry and hot, give the planting site a thorough soaking before you do anything else. Examine the root-balls and water these also if they have become dry during the journey. Early April is also a good planting time, as the soil will still be naturally moist.

Digging the hole After the water has soaked through, the planting hole for each can be dug out to a depth and width which will take the root-ball comfortably; ensure that the soil-mark on the stem is level with the soil surface. In general a saucer-shaped hole is ideal, and if the plant is slightly high, it is better than being planted too deep. Lining

The ideal time to plant new shrubs is in early April. Dig a saucer-shaped hole, ensure that both the soil and root-ball are moist, remove container, then plant so the soil-mark is level with the surface. Replace soil.

the hole with peat or leafmould will give the roots a very good start.

Planting Position the plant so that it is in the centre, with its best side facing to the front, and then crumble soil in round the roots to half-fill the hole while holding the plant steady; shake it a little to settle the soil and continue to add more fine soil, for preference using the topsoil until the hole is filled.

Then tread in the plant and soil, and fill in the resulting hollow, finishing with another good firming. Rake lightly, and spread a mulch at least 5cm (2in) deep, more if possible, of peat, 'Forest Bark' Ground and Composted Bark, or leafmould, over the surrounding soil so that the roots and some of the soil are covered. Make sure that this mulch does not touch the main stem.

TRANSPLANTING

Sometimes it is necessary to transplant, and remove a rhododendron or azalea to another position in the garden, because it has outgrown its old one, or because the site is needed for a different plant. Sometimes it is a case of colour clashes!

Preparation Whatever the reason, choose a day in autumn – the earlier in that season the better – when the soil is moist and rain is forecast. Dig out the new hole in advance, as for normal planting, and line it with humusy material of some kind, then lay polythene sheet over it to prevent any possible drying out.

First, mark a line round the plant on the soil at the furthest extent of the branches. Then tie the branches and foliage of the plant lightly together by wrapping a length of cord round them, gradually folding them neatly together.

Removal Then start to dig a trench along the line already marked, to a depth of about 23-30cm (9-12in), about the limit of most rhododendron roots. When the roots do not seem to go any deeper, work inwards beneath them all round the plant, stopping just short of the centre to leave the plant on a small platform. Push a spade underneath to tip the root-ball sideways a little, and chop off some of the roots and soil from the underside; do this all round the plant, finally cutting right under the platform to detach it completely.

Wrap the root-ball in sacking or wire netting for transport, and either carry it, by the root-ball, or drag it on a piece of canvas or plastic sheet to the new site, then plant as previously described.

CONTAINER GROWING

If you have alkaline soil in the garden, or if you don't have a garden at all, and you would dearly love to grown rhododendrons or azaleas, or both, there is an entirely satisfactory way round these difficulties. Growing in containers will allow you to grow any size completely successfully up to a height limit of about 2.1m (7ft).

They are ideal plants for container cultivation, as their fibrous roots naturally form a compact ball without penetrating deeply – maximum depth is little more than 30cm (1ft). Moreover, their beauty can be set off by the container; there are so many nowadays which will enhance the plants by reason of their shape, colouring and sculptured surfaces. If you use terracotta clay pots, look for those that are frost-resistant.

Whatever kind of container you use, there are two cardinal rules to planting in them. First, choose an acid compost. There are peat-based

Tie in all the branches to make transplanting easier. Carefully dig a trench round the shrub, as described in the main text, then wrap the root-ball before transporting.

proprietary composts which are specifically for ericaceous – acid-loving – plants such as rhododendrons, and an acid form of the John Innes soil-based potting compost. Second, make sure that the container is the right size; there should be about 4-5cm (1½-2in) to spare at the sides of the root-ball.

When planting, put a little moist compost in the base of the container; if it is clay, put some drainage material in first. Put the plant on this so that the soil mark on the stem is about 5cm (2in) below the rim of the container, then pack compost in down the sides until it just covers the root-ball surface; level it and water well.

11

AFTERCARE

To provide really first-class flowers, strong shoot growth and plenty of healthy well-coloured foliage, it is necessary to feed rhododendrons and azaleas regularly every year by providing bulky organic materials and by supplying granulated or powder fertilizers. You will remember that most of them grow naturally in a light woodland environment where the soil accumulates a deposit of rotting leaves and other vegetation that builds up constantly. Without it their fibrous roots, which are so near the surface, dry out rapidly and they are unable to absorb nutrients.

A raised bed is an attractive design feature in town and country gardens. It also provides a good solution to growing acid-loving shrubs in a garden where the soil is just the opposite. Keeping a small area at the right pH level is a relatively simple task.

A constant supply of organic matter is essential, and two good sources of this are peat and leafmould, provided the latter consists of leaves taken from trees growing in districts with acid soils. Others are bracken, once it has been heaped and rotted, garden compost which includes plenty of leaves, 'Forest Bark' Ground and Composted Bark, and well-rotted farm manure. A mulch 5cm (2in) deep of any of these materials can be applied in spring or autumn, spread over the area as far as the roots have reached. If the soil is light, use a thicker dressing.

Concentrated granular or powder fertilizers will give the plants the boost they need if put on towards the end of flowering, though they can also be applied any time up to early in mid summer for the majority. Slow-acting organic kinds are best,

as they supply nutrient for the rest of the growing season; they are expensive but need be applied at only 30-60g (1-2oz) per sq m (sq yd). They include bonemeal, for phosphorus, blood-fish-and-bone – the most convenient as it contains the most important nutrients: nitrogen, phosphorus and potassium as well as the trace elements – hoof and horn meal and dried blood which both provide nitrogen.

Pruning Pruning is not a chore that needs to be carried out regularly with rhododendrons and azaleas unless there are diseased or dead shoots or, occasionally, one which is growing much more strongly than the others. Such shoots should be cut out, well into healthy growth, with the cut made just above a leaf-joint. Otherwise they can be relied upon to grow into shapely plants of their own accord, increasing their shoot length by about 10-60cm (4-24in) a year, depending on the variety you have chosen.

Weeds and watering Weeds, particularly the perennial kind, should be kept clear of the area in which rhododendrons are growing. The time when they are establishing is especially important, and the dwarf varieties and smaller azaleas are also more vulnerable. Remove them while still small and easily hand-weeded or spot treat with 'Weedol'.

Rhododendrons must be kept well supplied with water during hot, dry sunny weather – the spring mulches will help here – and azaleas will probably need watering daily when flowering, or when growing in sunny positions. Use collected rainwater whenever possible, as it will be acid and at air temperature.

Container-grown plants will need feeding each year at the same season as the open-ground varieties. Also topdress them in autumn with fresh potting compost to replace the top 2.5cm (1in) or so of old, and to mulch in spring if not repotted.

Rhododendrons are rather particular about their soil conditions – and moisture requirements in dry spells – so a raised bed is an ideal location. Not only will it make the caring process easier, but it will also provide a pleasant sitting-out place if you incorporate a seat into the bed's architecture, as here. Grow a few scented azaleas at the front of the bed and you will double the benefits.

On the whole, rhododendrons and azaleas do not suffer much from infestations of pests or diseases. They are naturally healthy plants and more often than not, if infected at all, the problem does not become out of hand. But there are one or two troubles peculiar to them which can occur in some seasons, and if they are growing in a situation which is not reasonably suitable, again, they are more likely to be afflicted. The following are the problems most likely to occur.

Though some cultivars may be a little more resistant to bud blast, with so many possible carriers of the infection, it is wise not to count on getting such a plant. Follow the treatment recommended (right) the moment you see any sign of trouble.

Honey fungus (*Armillaria mellea*) This disease can infect any woody plant, not just rhododendrons and azaleas. A plant which stops producing new growth, gradually becomes pale green and then yellow all over, with limp leaves, can be suspected of being infected. If there are black strands like string in the soil near and among the roots, with white fan-shaped fungal growth on the wood just below the bark at soil level, the disease is present. Yellow toadstools at soil level in summer or autumn will confirm it. Affected plants can be treated with a proprietary phenolic emulsion if not too far gone, or removed completely, roots and all, and burned. Then either dig out the soil and replace with fresh or try sterilizing it with 'Clean-Up'. Do not replant in treated soil for at least eight weeks.

Lime-induced chlorosis Occurs when plants are grown in chalky soil, when the youngest, tip leaves turn yellow first, then the older ones. Water the plants with sequestered iron as the makers direct.

Red spider mite A minute pest which sucks the sap from leaves, living on their underside and spinning webs; it is most likely in hot dry conditions. The adult mite itself is brownish red and its feeding produces a greyish yellow speckling on the leaves. For prevention, always keep the plants well supplied with water, and spray overhead with water in hot weather. Spray with 'Sybol' at first sign of attack.

Rhododendron bud blast Flower buds turn brown and die, and in the following early summer black hairs develop on the surface; these produce spores which freshly infect the new season's buds. Buds browned by frost will not sprout such hairs. Wind, rain and leaf hoppers are thought to spread the spores. Pick off infected buds and spray with Bordeaux mixture or Benlate + 'Activex' in spring and thereafter continue to spray at 4-week intervals as a protectant.

Rhododendron leafhopper (Rhododendron bug) Small greenfly-like hopping insects whose young feed by sucking sap from the underside of leaves mainly near the ends of shoots from spring to late summer. Spray in late summer and early autumn with 'Picket' or 'Sybol'.

Weevils Small black or beige insects which feed on the young leaves near the soil, making characteristic small notches on the edges; feeding is nocturnal. The larvae are small white maggots which live in the soil and feed on the roots during autumn, mild weather in winter and early-mid spring. Dust or water with HCH (BHC), or spray plants and soil regularly with 'Sybol'.

Azalea leaf-gall Occasionally seen; young leaves thickened, with whitish grey bloom, flowers thickened and discoloured. Pick off affected parts and destroy. Spray with a copper-based fungicide.

Lime-induced chlorosis.

Vine weevil damage to rhododendron.

PROPAGATION

The easiest ways to increase rhododendrons and azaleas are by layering, by cuttings, and by seed. Plants produced by all of these methods can be exactly like their parents, even from seed, provided the latter has been 'selfed', that is, the pollen from one flower has fertilized the stigma of the same or another flower on the same plant – rhododendrons are self-fertile. But cross-pollination between species, varieties or hybrids produces entirely new individuals.

Even if you have not propagated a shrub before, you should find the layering method is reliable. Dig a shallow trench, sloping away from the shrub and with a straight 'back' furthest away. Prepare the chosen shoot as described in the text, then peg it down into the trench. Bend the end of the shoot upwards against the straight 'back' and support tip with a cane. Water well, then fill in the trench. Detach from parent plant only when rooting system is well established.

Layering This is the easiest method, and one of the most reliable. In spring, choose a one- or two-year-old shoot near to the ground; underneath it fork the soil and mix in peat and a little hoof-and-horn, or some proprietary peat-based potting compost. Make a slanting cut partially through the shoot, beneath a leaf-joint. Make a hollow in the soil immediately below, fill it with sand, and peg the layer down into the sand with forked sticks. Gently bend the end of the shoot upwards – don't force it because if you do it will break – and tie it to a cane. Water well, and cover the sand with more soil or compost. By autumn it will have rooted, but leave until there is plenty of root – this may be 18 months from the time of first layering. Then detach and transfer to a nursery bed until it is sufficiently developed for permanent planting.

Cuttings Both rhododendrons and azaleas can be grown from heel cuttings taken from about mid-June until about four weeks later. You are much more likely to be successful with the small-leaved than the large-leaved ones, so azaleas in particular can be easily reproduced in this way.

Use one-year-old sideshoots which have finished lengthening, but which are not yet woody right to the tip. Pull them off so that a 'heel' is left – a sliver of wood on the end from the parent plant – and remove the lower leaves from the 'cutting'. Fill a 9cm (3½in) pot with compost and make a hole at the side with a pencil. Insert the end of the cutting into a rooting compound, shake off the surplus, then place it in the hole so that the base rests on the compost and firm it in. Continue in this way round the edge of the pot, inserting cuttings. Then water them with a fine spray before covering with a polythene bag, raised clear of the seedlings on canes. Secure round the rim, and put the pot in a warm, shaded place. Expect rooting in about four weeks' time.

Seed You should be able to collect the seed in early winter ready for sowing a few days later. Collect the pods on as dry a day as possible, leave them to dry on a sheet of newspaper in a shed or similar place and, when they start to split, shake the seed out on to paper, and free it from husks. Then sow on the surface of peat-based seed compost, water very gently with a fine spray, and cover with plastic sheet. Keep in a temperature of 16-18°C (60-65°F). The young seedlings can be potted into cell trays when large enough to handle, and after further potting, planted in a nursery bed 18 months after germination.

Taking cuttings is most successful when they are taken from small-leaved rhododendrons and azaleas. Take them from about mid June to mid July, preparing them as described in main text. If you do try to propagate from a large-leaved plant, cut the leaves in half to reduce water loss until roots form.

VARIED AND VERSATILE

Rhododendrons and azaleas are among the most versatile of shrubs. Their tremendous variation in size, from tiny shrublets to trees 12m (40ft) and more high, means that they can be used in many situations in the garden. Moreover, they come in a rainbow of colours, including wonderful blues as well as yellows, oranges and scarlets.

Even a small border has sufficient room for one or two of the smaller rhododendrons or azaleas. The colour choice is also wide, so you should have no problem in planning a harmonious planting, whatever companion plants you decide to grow with them.

General garden planting The average height of a rhododendron is 90cm-2.4m (3-8ft), and width may be two-thirds to as much again when long established. As they are long-lived plants, it pays to choose a site carefully, though transplanting is not difficult, provided you have help.

Often, they are planted in groups, and indeed whole shrubberies may consist of them, but this does mean that you will have to choose several different varieties to avoid having a heavy bank of dull green for 11 months of the year. You can extend the flowering season of rhododendrons from early spring through to well into early summer. For instance, 'Praecox' has pink-lilac flowers in early spring; 'Diane', yellow flowers in mid spring and 'Britannia', red, in late spring; there are many other combinations for succession that could be chosen.

The small to medium rhododendrons and azaleas will fit well into a mixed border of herbaceous plants, bulbs and other shrubs. Blend the colour of their flowers with those around them at the same season, and put the taller varieties at the back. Lighten these with such tall and graceful herbaceous plants as the plume poppy (macleaya), the Russian sage (*Perovskia atriplicifolia*), hybrids of mullein (verbascum), or the giant 2.1m (7ft) foxtail lilies (eremurus), to provide contrast in form and flowers after the rhododendrons shed their blooms.

For the front of beds and borders the azaleas are more appropriate; many are quite small, round about 60cm (2ft), and have a much more delicate appearance, with their twiggy shoots, less crowded flower trusses and paler leaves. Some are deciduous.

Pink, yellow, orange, salmon, cream and all possible shades between these colours are one of the delights of azalea hybrids, and making a choice is always difficult. Go and see them in flower at nurseries, or in parks and specialist gardens, to give you an idea of the wide range available. Then mix your plants with autumn- and winter-flowering heathers, the miniature early spring-flowering bulbs – scillas, miniature daffodils, species tulips – or the summer-flowering carpeting campanulas such as *C. carpatica* or *C. porschaskyana*.

If you would like a collection of rhododendrons planted in one place, an area intersected with grassy, winding paths would break up the bulkiness of the plants. 'Temple Belle', forming a mound, with pink flowers; *augustinii*, blue flowers and growing to 4.5m (15ft), and the spreading white-flowered *R. quinquefolium*, an azalea, provide contrasts in shape, as well as flower colour, and the paths would allow them to be enjoyed from several different view points.

Rhododendron quinquefolium is a small Japanese form, deciduous and bearing its white flowers in April and May. This delicate charmer also has unusual foliage, the light-green, rounded leaves being edged with pale mauve.

Salmon-pink *Azalea* 'Betty' dips its flowers low over a path in the dappled sunlight of this woodland scene – perfect conditions for all of the rhododendrons and azaleas.

Woodland planting The most magnificent stands of rhododendrons can be found in woodlands, which is not surprising since many of them need shade for about half the day. In such an environment they are also supplied automatically with the humusy soil they need, as the autumn leaf-fall of deciduous trees round them rots into the soil. The moisture vital to their shallow, fine roots is retained by this organic material, and nutrient is returned, so that a natural cycle is set up.

The soil must, of course, always be acid, and a pH of 5.0 is the ideal – a range of between 4.0 and 6.5 will, however, be acceptable.

Trees to associate with rhododendrons and azaleas should not be thirsty species, such as sycamore or beeches, but instead the Scots pine, cedars and oaks. The snowdrop tree (halesia) and the pocket handkerchief tree (davidia) are further possibilities. Ornamental garden trees are good as well, as they do not grow too tall and consequently have less far-reaching roots. *Magnolia grandiflora*, Japanese maples, the sweet gum (liquidambar) and *Parrotia persica* are just a few examples of these.

Some rhododendrons will provide shade themselves in due course, growing to heights of 9-12m (30-40ft). Given some shelter from the sun while young, *R. arboreum* and *R. sinogrande* will eventually become flowering trees in their own right, and smaller species and hybrids can safely be planted in their lee if you should wish to do so.

In such situations rhododendrons can be allowed to naturalize and grow into one another. Slopes can be terraced with paths along them alternating with banks of rhododendrons and azaleas. Pools, moist boggy areas and streamsides lend themselves to Himalayan primula plantings, bordered by rhododendrons, themselves providing the combination of light and shade that these primulas also love.

Such a woodland site, with slopes and with some areas open to the sky, allows the most scope for rhododendron and azalea planting, when they can be given full rein to grow as they will, in association with each other and other plants. Embothrium, the South American flame of the forest, will enjoy the same environment, and wisteria can be seen at its magnificent best if it is allowed to romp freely over and up the taller and more wide-spreading kinds.

With its magnificent blue and white-tinted lavender flowers in 60cm (2ft) long racemes, the cultivar 'Multijuga' is a glorious sight in full flower and would be spectacular associated with the waxy orange-yellow tubular flowers of *R. cinnabarinum*.

When rhododendrons are planted in woodland, and left to their own devices, inevitably they will start to self-seed. You may find, therefore, that some startling new hybrids result, but in any case the natural effect of the original planting will be enhanced. If the conditions are entirely to the plants' liking, do not plant what is now known as the wild rhododendron, *R. ponticum*, with pretty purple flowers. It will self-seed with joyous abandon, swamping all your other plantings, and it is almost impossible to eradicate once it has become well established.

The lovely tubular flowers of *Rhododendron cinnabarinum* are a sight to behold in May and June. A choice Himalayan species that can become quite a large shrub.

Rhododendrons for specimen planting Banks of rhododendrons in full flower are a glorious sight, but if you plant a single variety, once the brief flowering season is over, many are undeniably nothing more than a block of dull green. However, some of them do have attractive leaves, such as the species *R. fulvum*, whose rose-pink flowers are set off by leaves with thick felt-like cinnamon-coloured hairs on the underside.

*Rhododendron sinogra
nde* is another good foliage species whose gigantic leaves are 75cm (30in) long and 30cm (1ft) wide, with whitish grey hairs underneath. Together with the flowers, which are creamy yellow, they help to lighten the whole bush in or out of flower. The young shoots have the same silvery white colouring, thus adding to the effect.

With its height of 6m (30ft) plus, sinogrande would make a superb specimen for woodland, planted where it could be viewed across a clearing, or on a slight hillock isolating it from other varieties.

Many other rhododendrons will similarly make a greater impact if planted singly. It is actually easier to take in the beauty of their flowers if you only have one to contemplate.

A well-chosen trio by anyone's standards: *Rhododendron* 'Brocade' and *Camellia* 'Donation' (a very popular variety), with the much smaller *Azalea* 'Hatsugiri' in the foreground. The variations in height ensure that each shrub gets its fair measure of attention, even in a group.

Rhododendron 'Temple Belle' is as delightful as the name and well deserves a prime spot in the garden in which to display the clusters of pink, mid-spring flowers. The blue-green leaves provide a perfect foil for the massed blooms.

The hybrid called 'Temple Belle' is a delightful example of a small rhododendron forming a mound of almost round leaves, blue-green coloured, decorated with clusters of pink bell flowers in mid spring.

Another specimen of quite a different kind would be 'Purple Splendour', an outstanding late-flowering rhododendron. The deep purple flowers have black spots in the throat, and are borne in clusters that completely cover the shrub. Each flower is so perfect and exquisite that even one plant is almost too much to take in; a group of them would have the effect of overkill and create a feeling that there was a lot of purple about.

By planting as specimens, rhododendrons are allowed to make the most of themselves. One of the places where they draw most attention is in a lawn, but the actual position there needs to be chosen carefully. You can make it a focal point which attracts the eye to one end of the lawn; a medium-sized hybrid such as the red-flowered 'Elizabeth', or the species *R. concatenans,* apricot, would be outstanding for such a position. Or you could put the plant in the centre of the lawn, provided that it will not break up a good sweep of lawn and look like a candle on a birthday cake. Alternatively, you can plant to one side or, if the lawn is an irregular shape, fit the plant into a bay formed by a curve, or into a corner.

Another way to use specimens is at a bend in a path, where the surprise felt on seeing them will double their impact and can literally stop viewers in their tracks. Corners between walls or fences are often good sites for a single plant, providing shelter from wind, and shade at some time of the day, as well as drawing attention to it, and filling what might have been an awkward site with something attractive.

Even if space is at a premium, you can still grow rhododendrons and azaleas. Thanks to their shallow root system, they can be accommodated even on a window-sill if you choose small species. And if you can go one better, with a small raised bed, then the choice is considerably increased. When planting within a wooden compound, as here, treat the timber with a wood preservative before planting up.

Containers, patios and terraces
You may or may not be reduced to gardening on a strip of paving outside the sitting-room; you may have a wide terrace with ample room for containers, or you may even only have a balcony or window-sill. But such areas lend themselves admirably to container cultivation, particularly of rhododendrons and azaleas, whose root-system is naturally compact and shallow.

The job of choosing suitable specimens is a pleasant one, because there are sizes from 30cm (1ft) to 1.5-1.8m (5-6ft), and you will be mainly limited here by the size of the container. Colour choice is a vast one, too, and you will be particularly hard put to prefer one of the dwarf azaleas to another, so dazzling are their colours. A third decision to make is on the type and design of container most appropriate.

Once upon a time we were mostly limited to terracotta clay containers, though there were also moulded Italian lead troughs and sculpted stone urns for those who preferred something different. Now the materials and designs available have expanded enormously, and continue to do so. There are containers made of reconstructed stone, cement, timber, glass fibre – coloured and moulded to look like the Italian originals – plastics of all kinds and colours, and clay itself. The production of pottery containers is now being revived as an art, and the old Victorian designs can once again be obtained.

Troughs, pots, tubs, urns and barrels are the main types, with pots particularly varying in design. If clay containers are chosen, however, make sure that they are guaranteed frostproof before you buy.

South-facing patios and terraces can receive blazing sun all day in summer, making them very hot. For such situations, choose the species or hybrids that actually like sun, and keep them very well supplied with water. To keep the roots cool, stand other containers of low-growing plants in front of them, or put them in another larger container and pack peat in the space between the two.

East- or west-facing paved areas which have periods of shade or sun during the day are ideal. North-facing sites are likely to be windy and several degrees lower than elsewhere but, provided they have shelter to the north not too far away, are still suitable.

Containers can be grouped, or placed singly; they can be sited in the angle between walls or along the foot of a wall. They can be placed at different levels in a collection by using pedestal urns, bricks, and staging of the kind supplied for conservatories. If there is a pool or waterfall close by, rhododendrons will form an especially attractive feature with it, and will benefit from the humidity resulting from the water.

Use any of the dwarf azaleas such as the Kurume hybrids, and the smaller rhododendrons: Blue Tit, *R. campylogynum* and the *yakushimanum* hybrids, which include the Snow White series of dwarfs. *R. yakushimanum* itself is taller, at 1.5m (5ft) but still suitable for large containers; so are 'Fabia' and 'Elizabeth' at 2m (6½ft), and 'Bow Bells' at 1.2m (4ft).

ABOVE In a small, sunny garden, variegated hostas provide protection when the sun is at its height, and their cream-edged foliage is a marvellous foil for more colourful plantings.

RIGHT
Rhododendron yakushimanum hybrid with deepest pink buds opening into pure white blooms.

Rock gardens One of the most attractive positions in which to grow the smaller rhododendrons and azaleas is a rock garden. It is not surprising that they lend themselves well to such surroundings, when you consider that they are often found growing on bare, rock-strewn hillsides which, incidentally, very often receive the full force of tropical sun.

Considerable humidity alleviates the latter, however, and there will be frequent heavy rains at certain times of the year ensuring water reserves deep down. In consequence, the roots of the plants may elongate much more than normal, but the rocks themselves will provide a cool root-run and prevent evaporation of moisture, and a well-constructed rock garden will be able to simulate the same sort of conditions.

Whatever the size of your rock garden, there are rhododendrons and azaleas of a size to suit. *R. scintillans* slowly grows to about 1m (3½ft), and is a mass of blue-purple flowers in spring. It naturally grows on moorlands in the Himalayas at high altitudes, and is tough, hardy, and beautiful. The prostrate *R. forrestii* has scarlet bell-shaped flowers in mid spring and will slowly form mats of evergreen shoots, sometimes up to 30cm (1ft) tall.

Other rhododendrons include 'Pink Drift', profusely flowering in rose pink; Blue Tit with lavender blue flowers which cover the plant, and any of the Snow White dwarf hybrids of *R. yakushimanum*. A good yellow species is *R. lepidostylum*, especially as it also has blue-green, almost metallic looking foliage. See also pages 30-33.

Kurume *Azalea* 'Palestrina' is one of the prettiest varieties in a notably attractive group. It is also an evergreen, so it will earn its place in the smaller garden; fully hardy.

The flowers of *Rhododendron* 'Orange Beauty' are so densely packed that it is almost impossible to see the foliage; a variety that really lives up to its name.

Whatever you choose, the plants will only look their best if you supply the right growing conditions. If you are building the rock garden from scratch, make certain that the drainage is first-class, with a good foundation layer of broken brick, broken clay pots and similar materials. These should be covered with turves laid upside down, and then with a growing medium similarly well-drained, whether it is a proprietary or home-made acid compost, or good garden loam, also acid, containing some grit.

The rocks should be placed to suggest outcrops, valleys and groups with their strata aligned as they would be in nature, thus ensuring that there are spaces in which the plants can grow, and appropriate conditions for each, perhaps with a little shade, a cool root-run or shelter from wind. Along with the rhododendrons, you can grow other plants which like acid soil, such as heaths and heathers, the creeping gaultherias or some of the small, heather-like daboecias.

Dwarf azaleas are superb for the rock garden. They are neat little shrubs, more wide spreading than tall, and they grow slowly, a few cm (in) every year. The Japanese evergreen hybrids are the ones from which to make a selection if you would like some leaf interest to remain after the flowers. Within this group, the Kurume azaleas are supreme. Most are single-flowered, but some are 'hose-in-hose'; that is, there appears to be one flower protruding from another. 'Blaauw's Pink', the white 'Palestrina' and the salmon-orange 'Orange Beauty' are among the prettiest.

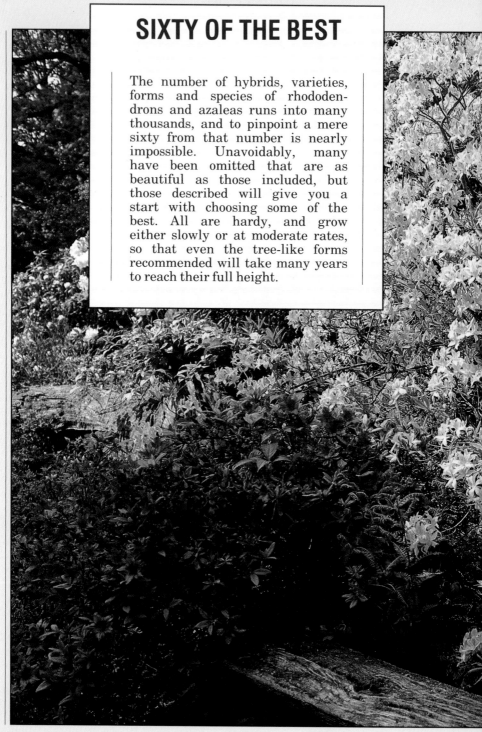

SIXTY OF THE BEST

The number of hybrids, varieties, forms and species of rhododendrons and azaleas runs into many thousands, and to pinpoint a mere sixty from that number is nearly impossible. Unavoidably, many have been omitted that are as beautiful as those included, but those described will give you a start with choosing some of the best. All are hardy, and grow either slowly or at moderate rates, so that even the tree-like forms recommended will take many years to reach their full height.

SMALL RHODODENDRONS
up to 90cm (3ft) tall

'Bashful'
One of the new hybrids of *R. yakushimanum*, in the Snow White dwarfs collection; deep pink, with a reddish brown blotch, open-funnel-shaped flowers, in clusters in late spring. Bush compact and rounded, to about 60cm (2ft). This variety needs some shade.

Blue Tit
A hybrid with two blue-flowered parents, *R. augustinii* and *R. impeditum*. Blue-purple, open flowers in twos and threes, backed by light green leaves. Forms a low-growing, densely spreading plant slowly reaching 90cm (3ft), more in ideal conditions. Flowers in mid spring, and does best where it is in shade for some of the day.

R. campylogynum
The characteristic colour of this species from the Chinese Himalaya, is a rich, deep purple, but in the wild it varies from rose-pink to such a deep purple as to be almost black, and white and even salmon-orange have been found. You will need to specify the colour when ordering. It forms a dense, neat mound eventually up to about 50cm (20in) tall, and more wide, making it a good rhododendron for the rock garden. Flowers in late spring and will grow in full sun.

'Doc'
Another of the Snow White *yakushimanum* hybrids; this is a charming, very pale pink hybrid, changing to white as it matures. The open-funnel-shaped flowers have a frilled edge, and open in clusters covering the bush; height is about 60cm (2ft). Flowering season is late spring and early summer. Provide shade from hot sun.

Rhododendron Blue Tit

Rhododendron yakushimanum 'Doc'

Rhododendron campylogynum in the full glory of its spring flowering

R. ferrugineum

This is the Alpen Rose of Switzerland, but it is a native of the European Alps as a whole, and of the Pyrenees, where it can easily cover vast areas of mountainside and where it flowers in midsummer. The flowers are small for a rhododendron, about 2cm (¾in) long, in clusters of up to 12, deep rose-pink to almost red, covering the bush in early summer. The underside of the leaves is covered in a thick indumentum (hairs) of rusty brown; grows into a dense rounded mound about 90cm (3ft) tall, on a sunny site.

R. forrestii

A small, creeping plant, once called *R. repens*, literally growing only a few cm (in) high, and able to cover the ground with mats of evergreen foliage consisting of rounded deep green, shining leaves about 2.5cm (1in) wide. This is a Chinese rhododendron from the north-west that grows at very high levels of 3000m (10,000ft) and more, and is an excellent species for a rock garden. Deep red wax-like flowers in ones, twos and threes appear in mid to late spring. A cool root-run beneath rocks is ideal.

Rhododendron yakushimanum 'Marion Street' has frilled flowers

R. lepidostylum

This species can easily be grown just for its beautiful blue-green, rounded leaves. A rounded mound about 60cm (2ft) high ultimately, it has pale to deep yellow flowers with dark spotting in the throat, appearing singly or in twos and threes in early summer, making it one of the later flowering species; it is also of Chinese origin. Does best where it receives a little shade.

'Marion Street'

Bred by Fred Street, this is another *yakushimanum* hybrid, and has the characteristic frilled flowers – this time in deep pink – appearing in late spring. As well as being one of the more suitable hybrids for edging or rock garden planting, it is a neat and pretty plant for containers.

'Pink Drift'

As with many of the smaller rhododendrons, the flowers are in twos or threes, but there are so many of these small clusters that the plant can be covered in flowers in late spring. Their lilac-pink trumpets emerge from a small dense bush about 60-75cm (2-2½ft) tall; out of flower it presents an olive-green appearance, darker than average.

R. scintillans

In the wild, in its native habitat in north-west China, R. scintillans grows to about 1m (3½ft), but in cultivation is likely to be less, and in any case is not a speedy grower. Flower colour can range from pale purple-blue to a much more intense true blue, but whatever shade it is, the plant is always extremely ornamental. The 4cm (1½in) wide flowers are wide open, almost like stars, in handsome clusters of up to six, during mid spring.

'Sneezy'

The third and last of the Snow White series of *yakushimanum* hybrids to be described here, 'Sneezy' exhibits the same neat round habit, and frilly-petalled flowers. The colour is a rose-pink, pale towards the centre, but with a deep red blotch on the upper part of the flower, which appears in late spring.

'Venetian Chimes'

Unusually for a *yakushimanum* hybrid, this is scarlet-flowered, making a dazzling display in late spring. It also has light green leaves, and a slightly more erect growth habit. In its parentage, it has R. *eriogynum*, bright red; Fabia, mixtures of orange and pink; and Fabia 'Tangerine', light red to a very attractive orange.

'Volker'

These *yakushimanum* hybrids, which have recently been bred and introduced, are ideal for patio and terrace planting, rock gardens, or where very small, neat, easily-grown and floriferous rhododendrons are wanted. The light yellow flowers of this hybrid have a red blotch at the base of each; late spring sees their main display. Raised by the German breeder Herr Hobie in Germany.

Rhododendron 'Sneezy', one of the Snow White series

MEDIUM-SIZED RHODODENDRONS
90cm-2.4m (3-8ft)

Blue Diamond

The size of this plant varies; it can reach about 2.1m (7ft), but it may remain at about 90cm-1m (3-3½ft); particularly good soil conditions will encourage the larger plants. Deep blue flowers, with a bias towards the purple side of blue, occur in clusters of five or so, and are nearly 5cm (2in) wide, being virtually without a tube. In mid spring the somewhat rounded bushes will be covered in flowers, hiding the small aromatic leaves. A sunny position is preferred.

Bowbells

A particularly delightful pre-war Rothschild hybrid with *R. williamsianum* as one of its parents, it has several attractive qualities. The young leaves and shoots are bronze, the buds are carmine red and the flowers a wide open funnel shape, bright but pale pink, carried six to a cluster. Plants usually reach about 1.5-1.65m (5-5½ft) in height in due course. A little shade is preferred.

'Britannia'

The vividly-scarlet, open bell-shaped flowers of this hybrid, introduced just after the First World War, are 7.5cm (3in) wide, in larger clusters of up to 14 in each. Although more than half a century old, this is still one of the best and most popular of the medium-height hybrids, and deservedly so. A position with some sun and some shade will ensure plenty of flower and a good leaf colour.

R. concatenans

One of the most charming of rhododendrons; the bell-shaped flowers are an outstanding pale orange-yellow, in clusters of about half-a-dozen, in mid to late spring. The new leaves are an unusual luminous green on their upper surface. Height is eventually 2.1-2.5m (7-8ft); some shade during the day will ensure the best colouring of the leaves.

Rhododendron 'Bowbells'

Rhododendron concatenans

Rhododendron 'Goldsworth Yellow' flowers are apricot in bud

Elizabeth

Introduced in 1933, Elizabeth quickly collected an Award of Merit and a First Class Certificate from the Royal Horticultural Society for its massive show of brilliantly scarlet flowers in mid spring. Each funnel-shaped flower is 7.5cm (3in) wide. Elizabeth can spread very widely to 1.8m (6ft) in each direction, with a height of about 1.2-1.5m (4-5ft), but will grow taller in a shady place. Growth is slow, even for a rhododendron.

Fabia

There are various forms of this hybrid, as the parents involved in the cross have been used many times, and the resulting plants have differently coloured flowers. Mostly they are shades of apricot, salmon and orange, with pink and copper overtones. The funnel-shaped flowers are in clusters of up to 10, from late spring to early summer. Height is also variable, between 90cm and 1.8m (3 and 6ft). A little shade improves the flower colouring.

'Goldsworth Yellow'

The yellow rhododendrons tend to be a little temperamental, but this is one of the most reliable, as might be expected of one of the older hybrids. It is a pale yellow-flowered hybrid with brown spots in the throat of a bell-shaped funnel flower; clusters may have 16 flowers in them, covering a 2.4m (8ft) bush in May.

Rhododendron 'Purple Splendour' has funnel-shaped flowers

'Mrs Furnivall'

One of the older, hardy, large-flowered hybrids from 1920; flowering in late spring, the colour is light pink, emphasized with a prominent and distinctive marking of wine-red inside the upper part of the funnel-shaped flowers. Up to 14 blooms occur in a cluster, and it can be covered in these extremely attractive flowers. Height is 1.8-2.4m (6-8ft); it is very slow-growing.

Praecox

The name of this one gives away its flowering season; in sheltered, warm gardens it can be in flower in late winter, otherwise early spring is more likely, but it does not do well where frost collects — its beautiful rosy lilac flowers will be burnt brown at the edges or even entirely destroyed. Otherwise, it can be a mass of wide open flowers, about 4cm (1¾in) wide, in twos and threes. One of the prettiest and most popular rhododendrons, its final height will be 1.2-1.5m (4-5ft), sometimes a little more.

'Purple Splendour'

A magnificent rich, deep purple hybrid, with a large black blotch in the centre of an open-funnel flower 7.5cm (3in) wide, and frilled at the margins. It is quite outstanding in flower at the end of late spring, especially under a light canopy of trees. Its upright habit extends to about 2m (6½ft) when fully grown.

R. williamsianum

This western Chinese species is one of the 'uncharacteristic' rhododendrons in that the leaves are rounded and heart-shaped, bronze when young, and the 6.5cm (2½in) wide flowers are perfectly bell-shaped. These are a clear pale pink, produced in pairs in mid spring — and in greatest quantity when the plant is in a really sunny place. It is a slow-growing rounded species to about 90cm (3ft), or 1.2-1.5m (4-5ft) in ideal positions.

R. yakushimanum

Unusually, this is Japanese, from the island of Yakushimana in southern Japan. A delightful and feminine flower, the rosy pink buds open pale pink and gradually mature to pure white; each cluster has about 12 flowers in an open-funnel shape with frilly edges. The leaves are white-felted when young. Height is up to 1.5m (5ft), but width can be at least 2.1m (7ft). The Exbury form is smaller and slower-growing, with intensely pink buds.

Rhododendron yakushimanum, small, neat and slow-growing

LARGE RHODODENDRONS
above 2.4m (8ft)

R. arboreum
An imposing and tree-like species which reaches 12m (40ft) in its native Himalaya. Flowers vary in colour from white to pink, to scarlet; the paler the flowers the hardier they are. It may take 20 years to flower, but then has up to 20 in a cluster, in early spring. The leathery leaves are 10-20cm (4-8in) long, and covered in a thick white or brown indumentum on the undersurface.

R. augustinii
This is one of the most famous of the blue-flowered rhododendrons, but in the wild the flower colour varies between blue, purple, pink and white, with all shades between. The forms grown in general are selections which have then been hybridized, using those most intensely coloured. Height is between 1.2 and 3m (4 and 10ft), but again this is a variable characteristic, and it may eventually become much taller.

Rhododendron arboreum

'Betty Wormald'
An extremely popular rhododendron, and deservedly so. The 12-flowered clusters perfectly display the 10cm (4in) wide funnel-shaped flowers, frilled at the edges and coloured deep to pale pink with a prominent mass of crimson speckling on the inside of the upper part of the flowers, which appear in late spring. Height is about 2.4-3m (8-10ft) and spread slightly more. A little shade is preferred.

R. cinnabarinum
The rhododendron genus is so vast that it has been divided into sections called Series, and species with like characteristics grouped within each. This one is the type species of its Series, and has the characteristic tubular flowers, up to eight in a cluster. Their colour is a waxy light red to orange-red, and they appear in late spring on a plant between 2.4 and 3.6m (8 and 12ft) tall. Metallic, grey-green leaves complete the colour scheme.

Blue *Rhododendron augustinii*

Vigorous *Rhododendron* 'Cynthia'

Rhododendron 'Loder's White'

'Cynthia'

A really old hybrid dating from 1862, strong, and vigorous in growth, reaching at least 7.5m (25ft). The deep rose-pink flowers, dark spotted on the inside of the upper part, form large, dome-shaped clusters of 24 blooms, early in late spring. For general impact, it is hard to top.

'Damaris Logan'

The bell-shaped, bright yellow flowers of this choice hybrid are probably the best of their colour. There are between 6 and 12 flowers in a cluster, and in good conditions it can easily be covered in bloom in late spring. Height is 3m (10ft). A mild and sheltered garden will suit it best.

R. fulvum

A species which does not rely solely on flowers for its display; the leaves are large — to 20cm (8in) long — with a rich red-brown indumentum on the underside, easily seen as it matures, because it reaches a height of between 2.4 and 6m (8 and 20ft), forming a shrub or small tree. The bell-shaped flowers are white or pink, marked crimson at the base of the throat and borne in clusters of 20 which open during early spring.

R. griersonianum

Given sun and a position sheltered from wind, this unusual rhododendron will be seen at its best. The brilliant and unusually light red flowers are tubular, opening to a trumpet shape, in loose clusters of up to 12 in early summer. The leaf undersurface is pale brown, due to the woolly felt which covers it, and the entire plant tends to be covered in fine hairs or down. The shape is also most attractive, and final height can be 2.7 or 3m (9 or 10ft).

'Loder's White'

A hybrid raised in the 19th century, this is one of the most magnificent of the white-flowered rhododendrons, and probably has the white species *R. griffithianum* in its parentage, which also gives it a slight perfume. The buds are pink and the flowers funnel-shaped and large, 10cm (4in) wide, in conical clusters of 12, in late spring. Height can be 4.5m (15ft).

The most commonly planted of all – *Rhododendron ponticum*

'Pink Pearl'

Even non-gardeners have heard of this rhododendron hybrid, so well-known is it. It was first shown in 1896, and still continues to be much grown, a tribute to its strong constitution and beauty. Large upright clusters of 18 flowers unfold late in mid spring, to cover an upright plant up to 4.5m (15ft) tall. The deep pink-lilac, funnel-shaped flowers are large and frilly-edged, 10cm (4in) wide, becoming pale pink to practically white as they age. A sunny position will prevent it becoming leggy and bare at the base.

Rhododendron 'Pink Pearl'

R. ponticum

A native of the area round the Black Sea and the Balkans, Spain and Portugal, *R. ponticum* was introduced to cultivation in the mid 18th century. Its funnel-shaped, light purple flowers in late spring are a familiar sight in practically any garden where rhododendrons are grown, but it has taken to deliberate planting much too enthusiastically. It has now self-seeded large areas of woodland and moorland, and become invasive. So, although easily grown, it should be planted with caution, if at all. It is much used as a stock on which to graft hybrids; but if allowed to sprout, the stock takes over and accounts for the apparent change in flower colour which sometimes occurs. Height can be as much as 7.5m (25ft).

'Sappho'

Introduced before 1867, 'Sappho' is a delightful hybrid with large dome-shaped clusters of 15 flowers, 7.5cm (3in) wide, white with a deep purple-black blotch in the throat. Height is about 4.5m (15ft), and a sunny position will prevent it from becoming too leggy.

Rhododendron 'Sappho'

R. sinogrande

One of the outstanding characteristics of this species is the generally grey-silveriness of young leaves and young stems following the mid spring flower display. The flower colour varies from creamy white to yellow, blotched in the throat with crimson, and immense clusters of up to 30 bell-shaped flowers are produced. Height is eventually 10.5m (35ft) and it needs shelter from wind for its best display. The leaves are on the grand scale, too, being 60cm (2ft) or more long, and 30cm (1ft) wide.

R. thomsonii

One of the best species, *R. thomsonii* is a Himalayan rhododendron to about 4.5m (15ft) tall. It needs a little cossetting, otherwise the flowers are damaged by frost, but it is well worth a sheltered position with a little shade. Its waxy, deep red, bell-shaped flowers open in early to mid spring, in loose clusters of up to 10, backed by leaves with a bluish-white underside.

Rhododendron thomsonii has attractive bark, bell-shaped flowers

Azalea 'Irene Koster' is delightfully fragrant

DECIDUOUS AZALEAS

These hybrids are mostly derived from American species together with *R. luteum,* from the Near East, and *R. molle* and *R. japonicum* from the Far East. All have funnel-shaped flowers with long and prominent stamens.

'Berryrose'
The open trumpet-shaped flowers of this hybrid are spectacularly salmon pink with a deep yellow blotch in the throat and a reddish tube to the trumpet. Late spring is the usual flowering time and it is particularly profuse in flowering. The plant slowly grows to about 2m (6½ft).

'Floradora'
A late flowering azalea, towards the end of May, the colour of the flowers is a light orange-red, with a flare of brown spots in the throat. Height is between 1.2 and 1.5m (4 and 5ft), so it is a good plant for patios and terraces, especially as it gives its best display in a sunny place.

'Irene Koster'
Where a blend of delicate colours is required, 'Irene Koster' will fit in well, with its white flowers flushed a beautiful rose-pink; the longer-than-usual tube is crimson, and a yellow blotch marks the throat; strongly fragrant. Flowering time is early summer. Height is 1.5-1.8m (5-6ft).

'Koster's Brilliant Red'

In contrast to the preceding hybrid, this is a dazzling, vivid orange-red. In autumn, the leaves echo the flowers in shades of orange and red before they fall. The end of May sees the flowers unfold, on a plant about 1.5m (5ft) tall. Plenty of sun will ensure the best display.

R. luteum

One of the oldest of the cultivated rhododendrons, introduced even before *R. ponticum*, this is sometimes called the honeysuckle azalea, both from its appearance and its fragrance. It grows quickly to its ultimate height of 2.7-3m (9-10ft), and in a sunny place will be covered in golden flowers with longer than usual, protruding stamens in late spring. Your nose will tell you long before your eyes that there is a specimen nearby. The leaves change to dazzling shades of orange, red, crimson and purple in autumn. Easily grown, it will self-seed.

'Narcissiflora'

An unusual azalea in that it has a 'hose-in-hose' flower in which the stamens have been converted into petals to make the flower double. The colouring is beautiful, being a soft clear yellow in early summer, followed by attractively bronzed leaves in autumn. Fragrance completes the attractions of a plant ultimately 2-2.4m (6½-8ft) tall.

'Norma'

Another 'hose-in-hose' or double azalea, especially interesting in that there can be more than one main colour to the petals. The normal shade is a light coral red, but in some plants the converted petals are white; in both cases there are yellow markings on the inside of the upper lobes. It flowers mid to late May, and the fragrant flowers cover a plant that remains quite small – at 1.2 – 1.5m (4 – 5ft) tall.

'Persil'

This is a dazzling white as the name suggests, and it is all the brighter by contrast with the beautiful yellow flare on the inside of the upper lobe of its faintly scented, spectacular flowers. These are larger than most – at 6.5cm (2½in) wide – in clusters of about 20. Flowering time is late spring. Height is 1.5m (5ft).

Double *Azalea* 'Norma'

Azalea 'Persil', whiter than white

43

EVERGREEN AZALEAS

The evergreen hybrid azaleas are mostly derived from Japanese species and are sometimes simply known as Japanese azaleas. They are much more compact and low-growing, often wider than tall! Among them are the Kurumes, from which E. H. Wilson, a plant hunter early in this century, chose 50 he considered to be the best – the 'Wilson Fifty'.

'Addy Wery'

This has *R. kaempferi* as part of its parentage, and is a Kurume azalea, though not one of the 'Fifty' – it is a modern hybrid. In late spring, it is a sheet of brilliant vermilion red: the flowers are larger than most, being about 4cm (1½in) wide and the same length, and height is tall for an azalea, to about 1.2m (4ft) and sometimes as much as 1.8m (6ft). A little shade preserves the flower colour.

'Betty'

A beautiful deep dusky pink hybrid with a salmon tinge, the colour of this hybrid is intensified in the centre of the narrowly funnel-shaped flower. Opening in late spring, the plant gives its best flowering display in a sunny place. The upright growth matures at about 1.2-1.5m (4-5ft).

'Blaauw's Pink'

Another salmon pink, but with a more intense pink tone; it is a mass of flowers in mid to late spring, almost completely hiding the leaves. The flowers are 'hose-in-hose', thus intensifying the effect. A Kurume evergreen azalea, it is densely twiggy, to 90cm-1.2m (3-4ft) and rather more wide. Given a little shade, the flowers are more intensely coloured.

'Fedora'

'Fedora' is one of the most popular and widely grown azaleas, first introduced in 1922. It is a kaempferi hybrid and therefore one of the taller azaleas at 1.5m (5ft), though it will take many years to reach this height. It is flat-topped and spreading, and has large flowers more than 5cm (2in) wide, coloured deep rose-pink in late spring. It needs a completely sunny position to do itself justice.

Gumpo

There are several plants in this group. Their botanical origin is uncertain, but they are very prettily flowered plants with blooms more than 5cm (2in) wide, frilled at the edges. Gumpo Pink is pale, Gumpo or Gumpo White is all-white, and both are small plants slowly growing to about 60cm (2ft), spreading much more widely, to 90cm (3ft). They are part of the Kurume section, and are ideal for rock gardens where they have plenty of sun and a sheltered warm position. The flowering season for this variety is early summer.

Azalea 'Addy Wery'

The deep magenta flowers of *Azalea* 'Hatsugiri' are small but profuse

'Hatsugiri'

If you want something different in the way of colour, then this Kurume azalea will certainly provide it; the flower colour is a deep pure magenta, and so profusely produced are the flowers that the plant becomes a solid sheet of colour towards the end of late spring. The flowers are small, 2.5cm (1in) wide, but make up for this in their abundance. Height is 60–90cm (2–3ft). It is reliably hardy but needs a good sunny site in the garden for best flower production.

'Hinodegiri'

In 'Wilson's Fifty' this is No 42 – he gave it the English name of 'Red Hussar' – and it has brilliant red flowers early in late spring. In autumn the leaves are suffused with tints of orange, bronze and red and some will fall. This is because many of the evergreen azaleas lose their spring leaves, but by then will have grown a second set during summer which hang on until the spring or longer, when the new spring ones unfold. Size is just 60cm (2ft) but spread can easily be 1.5m (5ft).

'Hinomayo'

The number of medals this hybrid has been awarded vouch for its appearance and popularity – it has the Award of Merit, the Award of Garden Merit, and a First Class Certificate. A Kurume hybrid, it is one of the most easily grown but do not be surprised if most of the leaves fall in autumn. It is one of the least evergreen of this section of azaleas, but the new season's buds are quite safe. A pink to out-pink all others, one plant is quite sufficient if it is to be appreciated properly. Height is eventually about 90cm -1.2m (3-4ft), width another 60-90cm (2-3ft). Dappled shade is ideal.

Azalea 'John Cairns'

'John Cairns'

A red-flowered hybrid, but of such an unusual shade that it has been variously described as dark orange-red, Indian red, dusky terracotta, brownish red and deep red. It is of kaempferi stock, and flowers in late spring, making quite a large plant for an azalea, 1.5m (5ft) tall and as much wide. Some of the leaves change from green to scarlet in autumn and fall; those that last through winter turn brown and keep this colour. A little shade is advisable.

'Orange Beauty'

Another which has picked up a mass of awards, like 'Hinomayo', the true clear orange of this hybrid is unusual, since many so-called oranges have salmon, pink, yellow or red flushing or tinting to diffuse an otherwise pure colour. The flowers are slightly frilly, appearing late in mid spring on a plant slowly reaching 90cm (3ft) and rather more in spread. Some shade is necessary.

'Palestrina'

So many of the smaller azaleas are 'hot' colours of red, pink, orange, salmon and crimson-purple, that it is a relief to find one that is a refreshingly icy white, emphasized by green rays deep in its centre. To about 1.2m (4ft), tall rather than wide, it flowers in late spring, in sun. This is one of a collection of Vuyk hybrids introduced by a Dutch nursery from Boskoop in 1926.

'Rosebud'

A charming little azalea with very double 'hose-in-hose' rose-pink flowers, almost like roses, flowering in late spring. An American hybrid of comparatively recent introduction – it was given an Award of Merit in 1972 – it is widely distributed and easy to obtain. It has a spreading growth habit, and ultimate height is likely to be 1.5m (5ft). Dappled shade is required.

Double *Azalea* 'Rosebud'

'Silver Moon'
This recently introduced hybrid, also from America, flowers later than the white 'Palestrina' already mentioned, not until early summer, and needs to be planted in a warm and sheltered place in order to give of its best. Not hardy in colder areas. The white flowers are large, 6.5cm (2½in) wide, frilled at the edges and marked with pale green inside the upper part of the flower. Height is likely to be about 1.2m (4ft) when the shrub is fully mature. It also has a widely spreading habit.

'Vuyk's Scarlet'
Vuyk has already been mentioned in the description of 'Palestrina'; he was a Dutch hybridizer, who founded the nursery of Vuyk van Nes. Many lovely hybrids were distributed from this source, and 'Vuyk's Scarlet' was introduced in 1954. A good deep crimson colour, the frilly, funnel-shaped flowers appear in May, and totally cover a small but spreading plant. It is a good container plant, and ideal for the rock garden, too. A sunny place is preferred.

COLOUR SELECTION OF RHODODENDRONS

Red
arboreum
'Britannia'
cinnabarinum
forrestii
Elizabeth
griersonianum
thomsonii
'Venetian Chimes'
'Addy Wery'
'Floradora'
'Hinodegiri'
'John Cairns'
'Koster's Brilliant Red'
'Norma'
'Vuyk's Scarlet'

Orange
concatenans
cinnabarinum
Fabia
'Betty'
'Orange Beauty'

Yellow
'Damaris Logan'
'Goldsworth Yellow'
lepidostylum
sinogrande
'Volker'
luteum
'Narcissiflora'

White
arboreum
fulvum
'Loder's White'
'Sappho'
sinogrande
yakushimanum
Gumpo White
'Irene Koster'
'Palestrina'
'Persil'
'Silver Moon'

Purple
campylogynum
ponticum
Praecox
'Purple Splendour'
'Hatsugiri'

Blue
augustinii
Blue Diamond
Blue Tit
scintillans

Pink
arboreum
'Bashful'
'Betty Wormald'
Bowbells
'Cynthia'
'Doc'
ferrugineum
fulvum
'Marion Street'
'Mrs Furnivall'
'Pink Drift'
'Pink Pearl'
'Sneezy'
williamsianum
'Berryrose'
'Blaauw's Pink'
'Fedora'
Gumpo Pink
'Hinomayo'
'Irene Koster'
'Rosebud'

INDEX AND ACKNOWLEDGEMENTS

Picture credits
Pat Brindley: 4/5, 39(I).
Lyn & Derek Gould: 30(bl).
S & O Mathews: 1, 20, 28/9.
Harry Smith Collection: 12, 13, 15(l,r), 18, 19, 21, 22, 24, 25(t,b),
27, 32, 33, 34(bl), 36, 37, 38(r), 40(t).
Michael Warren: 6, 7(t,b), 14, 23, 26, 30(br), 31, 34(br), 35, 38(I),
39(r), 40(b), 41(t,b), 42, 43(l,r), 44, 45, 46(t,b).

Artwork by Simon Roulstone